The Art of the ETHICAL Deal

DEDICATION

This book is dedicated to all the high integrity business people who every day prove we all thrive at a higher level with win/win transactions.

CONTENTS

Introduction

Everything is advanced by a deeper acceptance and alignment with the truth.

This book focuses on what is true about deals. Some of the concepts may seem familiar and some of them certainly won't. I challenge you to ask yourself, "is this true?" when you encounter foreign ideas in the pages that follow.

In every chapter there are stories from my experience that illustrate the point being made. While they are unquestionably self serving, they are intended to be both illustrative and inspiring. As I wrote this I had in mind two truths I hold to be very important: Example is the most powerful form of leadership, and in order for others to think well of us, we must think well of ourselves.

I once asked a Rabbi, yes a real one, how to know where the line is between accepting and acting on our strengths and being arrogant or conceited. He told me as long as everyone is better off, I'm on safe ground.

With that said, you WILL be better at deals for having read this book. Enjoy!!!!

Chapter 1

Win/Win

"No one can sustainably benefit at the expense of others"
Scott Friedman

There is a win/win perspective that is honest in every deal worth doing.

In most deals the details of the win/win aspects for the participants are not fully clarified and accepted. There tends to be a superficial understanding, while the deeper value goes largely unrecognized and unappreciated. To some degree part of that deeper value doesn't occur precisely because it isn't recognized and appreciated. As always, the point is best illustrated with a story…

In my mortgage business, the superficial understanding of win/win is I earn a fee for assisting someone in obtaining a real estate loan.

Going a level deeper, I listen to my client's objectives and compassionately and effectively respond to their needs.

Going a level deeper, I use the mortgage business as a venue to care about others and for them to open their heart more as well to care about me. That's evident when my clients have told me they want to be sure I'm earning a fee when I do a no point no fee refinance for them. I explain the lender is paying the fee from a credit due to the fact they're paying an incrementally higher interest rate. I go over all the details with them and thank them for their concern I get paid (smile). All that is a physical expression of the care and respect we have for each other.

The next level deeper is we feel a deep trust of each other and the peace of mind that comes with that trust. I don't worry clients will drop me for someone willing to do the loan I've structured for $.50 less and they are confident I'll give my maximum effort to help them all I can and treat them fairly. They know I'll be responsive, committed and honest.

The deepest level is simply deepening our experience of peace and the sense of well being that is part of that peace. Another aspect of that peace and sense of well being is a sense of wholeness; a sense that we have everything we need; are not lacking anything, are complete.

When there is a recognition and appreciation of the value received and provided on all these levels, win/win is maximized. The value is present in every deal, and it is up to us to focus on, relate to, appreciate and benefit from our awareness of its existence.

Chapter 2

Components of Value

"Price is not the only component of value"
Scott Friedman

In every deal some things are more valuable and important to the parties than others. Rarely are people fully aware of all they value in a deal and the relative importance of twhat they value. The more we can be clear about what we value most, second, third, etc, and what the other parties to the deal value most, second, third, etc, the easier it is to put together a deal everyone is happy with.

The easiest and most sensible place to start is with our self. What do I value most, second, third, etc? For me, I value uplifting relationships where I feel stronger, more energized, more respected, more at peace, and happier as a result of the interaction. I like clients that are open, thoughtful, kind, responsive and appreciative as those characteristics seem to support me getting the outcome I want.

To uncover what my clients most value, I listen and ask the best questions I can. Especially in my initial meetings, I do my best to get to know them as people in addition to their role as clients. I take note of how they spend their discretionary time, the perspectives they use to explain situations and what they like to talk about. These are all clues to understanding what they value. If they're spending a lot of time with their grandkids, I know family is an important part of their life. If they're interested in politics, I know they feel personally affected by what's going on in the world and it matters to them. If they've had bad purchasing experiences in the past, I know greater articulation of the process will be helpful.

For some people who they're dealing with is very important. For them, who they work with must be someone they trust and respect. For others, they are primarily concerned with a smooth process that will consume as little of their time and attention as possible. Some start out thinking price is the only component of value, giving no consideration to long term cost, different product options that may better serve them, or even the ability to deliver on commitments. Sadly, some commit to deliver a mortgage without ever determining if the client qualifies for one. I once had a client that had only a few days to meet a 1031 exchange deadline. Obviously speed was the primary component of value there.

The more we can be clear about what we and others value, the easier we can put together a successful deal. I even had a client once who said he just had to do business with someone who would wear Mickey Mouse ears from Disneyland to a Town Council meeting (I thought it would be fun).

Most people value trust, competence and ease of doing business. Knowing that I make a point to be open, encourage questions, explain the process including timing and fill out as much of the paperwork for the client as possible.

In my experience when people feel they're being listened to and their priorities being taken into account, they'll provide all the information necessary to make a successful sale. All other things being equal, people will choose to do business with those they like and trust.

Chapter 3

It's Not Done Until It's Done

"A deal isn't a deal until the last check clears the bank"
Scott Friedman

Any deal can blow up, even at the very end. Too often people say and think, "it's a done deal" before it's over. Sometimes people will commit at the outset that this will be a smooth, problem free deal: big mistake!!!! Anything can happen.

The most destructive part of thinking a deal is done before it's done is when people think they can stop paying attention. It's attention to detail every step of the way that gets deals done. I prefer to say, "So far so good. I don't see any obstacles at this point, and I'll continue to pay attention until it's done". Not is it only more honest, and therefor more confidence inspiring, it also reaffirms my commitment to pay attention. **Attention is what it takes to get deals done.**

The unexpected can always occur. I've had title companies temporarily lose documents. The County of San Diego once had two different addresses for the same property in two different places in the county's records. After the 1994 Northridge earthquake (I've been doing this a long time….) lenders required a certificate from a state licensed engineer certifying the house was livable before they'd fund a loan in the San Fernando Valley. The Federal Reserve shut down for 2 days and no loans could fund after 9/11. Lenders have suspended funding loans when the subject house was in a fire area many times. Someone else's liens mistakenly appeared on a preliminary title report. Someone else's derogatory credit mistakenly shows up on a client's credit report. Once, I even had a borrower decide she didn't want to buy that specific house after she signed the loan documents and the lender funded the loan. These are just some of the unexpected hurdles that have appeared in deals I've done. As they say, "It's never over until it's over".

There are almost always adjustments or actions that must take place all the way through to the closing and final settlement of deals. I can't count the number of times I've said, "check, double check and re check again" to describe my actions to do everything in my power to see deals close smoothly. I even use an overnight carrier that sends me an e mail with the time and who signed for documents crucial to getting deals done.

Possibly the worst offense in assuming a deal is done before it's done is spending the money from the deal in advance. That puts huge pressure on getting the deal done, so much pressure that it usually limits effective and good decision making. Don't spend or commit funds not yet received!!!!!!

Remember, **"This is the real world, anything can happen".** I even had a client once ask with worry, "what if something happens to you?" Some risks are just unavoidable. I told her I'd be careful. Good news, nothing bad happened to me.

Chapter 4

Engagement and Trust

"One measure of maturity is our ability to see our self in others"
Scott Friedman

Nothing builds trust like being open and taking an interest in others. One of the most valuable of all skills is to find something about another that interests us and ask about it. It's a skill we all can improve on no matter how good or bad we're at it right now. Our interest must be sincere for the other person to feel heard, respected, valued and appreciated. When we feel that way towards them, they'll feel that way towards us.

Nothing happens without some degree of trust. The deeper the trust the more vulnerable and open people are willing to be. That opens the door to provide greater and greater value.

I was doing a loan for a long term client. He had the cash to close but didn't want to part with it because it was his reserve security. Because I've known him for close to 20 years I was comfortable making him an unsecured loan so he could keep his reserves and still close the deal. That trust allowed him to benefit from the better mortgage, replace high interest unsecured debt with lower interest unsecured debt, and deepen our trust and friendship. This would never be possible without trust.

Many of my clients have been with me for decades. When I call them up and tell them there is an opportunity to improve their position, they almost always say, "let's go". They don't worry that I'm scamming them. They don't worry about anything. They trust me based on years of experience. I even have to force them to pay attention when they sign final loan documents because they say, "I trust you". I go over the note and settlement statement with them in detail anyway.

I've lent money, both secured and unsecured, to people that could never have gotten those loans in the general market because I know and trust them. So far at least, they've all proved worthy of my trust (writing this better not jinx that!!). Most have already paid me back in full as agreed.

The title company I've worked with for about 25 years will do things for me because they trust me to follow through on my word. They've even taken personal checks from me, which if you know this business, almost never happens.

The more deeply engaged we are with people, the deeper the trust. The greater the trust, the more opportunity there is for deals of greater and greater value. Conversely, there are people I flat out will not do business with. Years ago I turned down a loan request telling the borrower he wouldn't be happy with me and I wouldn't be happy with him, so we weren't going to proceed. He was one of the those people who isn't happy with himself or anyone else. I trusted what I knew not to do a deal.

Chapter 5

Identify and Meet Needs

"If I have PEACE, I have everything of value"
Scott Friedman

Everyone has needs on a variety of levels. The most basic, fundamental and I believe deepest need is to be at peace; even deeper and more precious than love.

Because the most powerful form of leadership is example, the best way to help people experience peace is for us to be at peace. I once had an attorney who was referring business to me. I asked him why because I was curious. He said it was because I'm the only mortgage broker he'd ever met that was calm. All the rest seemed to him, to be nervous about something. Don't ever sell the practical benefit of being at peace short. I've had more than just that attorney comment how attractive it was to work with someone who was calm and straight. Think about it. When anyone, including us, is at peace, there are NO problems in that moment. That leads me to another favorite saying, **"If you don't mind, it doesn't matter"**. We all have a need to be free of our problems.

Everyone has a need to care and be cared about. I left one client telling him I'd do everything in my power to help him even though I didn't control all aspects of the deal. There was a warmth in that moment that inspired me to say, "I care about you". The warmth of that moment was palpable. He responded saying, "I know and I appreciate you". (beats the heck out of an adversarial relationship, don't you think?)

Filling the deeper needs in addition to the surface needs of providing a product or service that works for a fair price, creates loyalty. The deeper needs include being respected, valued, trusted, cared for and most of all, being at peace.

Our ability to meet the needs of others is a reflection of our ability to meet our own needs. We can't inspire peace and trust in others if we're not at peace with our self, if we don't trust our self. **We can't expect others to think well of us if we don't first think well of our selves.**

We all have the capacity to identify peace, love, integrity and empathy within ourselves. The more we identify, accept and relate to those qualities within our self, the more we can help others do the same. Often this is best done in the context of doing a deal. It's part of the need of every person in every deal.

Chapter 6

The Purpose of Business

"The only legitimate purpose of business is to support people" – Scott Friedman

Most of the time earning money comes as part of supporting people, although not always.

When people make money the sole purpose of business, they are willing to sacrifice everything else to get more money. They will misrepresent, they will pollute water to the point we can't safely drink, they will destroy others financially, they will blackmail people, they will steal, and they will renege on payment. We've seen all this and worse in our society.

The purpose of business is to create win/win exchanges in which everyone is better off. For those committed to zero sum thinking, this may seem impossible. In zero sum thinking there is only so much value and either I have it or someone else has it, but we both can't have more of what's worth having. They are committed to the notion that for every winner there is a loser, for every rich person there must be poor people and so on. They extend that thinking to money. Either they have it or someone else has it because there is only so much of it. I challenge zero sum thinkers to test out their assumptions. Is the supply of money static? Is a successful life measured in money or the experience of love, joy and peace? Howard Hughes' life proved money doesn't necessarily buy peace.

Money is one of many forms value takes. Ultimately **money is a tool** that only has value to the extent it supports our experience of love, joy and peace. If it doesn't do that, it's worthless. I use money to provide food and shelter for me, my wife and my dogs. That is an expression of and deepens my experience of love. Here, I'm willing to spend, give up money in exchange for a nice home for us. Our phone allows us to communicate and feel connected to people.

There is joy and peace in that connection, so I'm good with spending money for phone service.

During the crazy years of mortgage lending where it was easy for people to obtain loans they would not be able to pay back, I wouldn't do it. Even though I left a lot of money on the table, I refused to do loans people couldn't pay back. That would be hurting everyone including my own conscience. When it all crashed, I didn't need to go into hiding like so many others. I'm still in business while many others are not. There are always opportunities for good business that helps people and bad business that hurts people. It's up to us to choose.

Once I was doing a loan for a single man caring for his daughter with AIDS. We got down to the closing when he said, "I'm sorry, I just can't part with the money to pay your fee. I feel I need to keep it to pay for my daughter's medical care". I told him I was sure there was a win/win solution here and asked for the weekend to find it. Over the weekend I decided the warmth I would experience in forgoing my fee to honor his commitment to his daughter was more valuable to me than the fee. I did his loan for no dollar fee, and felt good about it. While all the other loans I've done for him, I've earned a fee, in this case good business did not include getting paid in dollars.

I haven't run my business life to maximize my dollar income. I've run it to enrich my life. I've been able to provide for my family, help my clients, have time for myself, my wife, my friends and my dogs. My own enrichment is reflected in increasing my value and contribution to society. I enjoy speaking at graduations, writing books and consulting with business people. Most of that I've been paid for, although not all. All of it enriches me and others, so it's good business.

Chapter 7

Gathering and Organizing Resources

"A solution to every problem exists if we have the energy to recognize and avail ourselves of it" - Scott Friedman

There are lots and lots of people and organizations that use resources at their disposal, to ingratiate themselves to clients that are both businesses and individuals. In general there are massive resources at our disposal. The limiting factor, as always, is our capacity to identify, accept and benefit from those resources.

I've found businesses that rely on me for business, friends and clients to be my best resources.

The title company I work with is always happy to review documents I've drawn up to insure they'll be acceptable to the county recorder and the title company. When I need to satisfy a lender condition of proving a client does not own a specific parcel, the title company provides the documentation at no charge.

My current primary lender contacts my clients they've funded loans for once a quarter on my behalf to remind them I exist. No charge.

Even an appraiser I worked with years ago will help me with comparable sales data as a favor. (Current law prevents me from selecting appraisers any more)

My good friend designs book covers for me. He sends out press releases for me.

A mortgage client who is a very successful author helps me with marketing my books.

I get encouragement, support and ideas from a great number of people. I'm also generous with my encouragement, help and support.

With all the help and resources that surround me, it is increasingly evident that I am the limiting factor in my growth and progress. I even have friends that help me with my growth. I'm fond of saying, "I never get lost, everyone tells me where to go".

There is security and confidence in accepting there is help for us. There is even help in opening up to and benefitting from help that in fact exists for us.

Chapter 8

Getting Help From Invested Parties

"When anyone is helped, we all are helped"
Scott Friedman

There are people in almost all of our lives who depend on us doing well. They could include our spouse, our clients, certainly the government (they want our tax money if nothing else), our friends count us to be there for them, children, parents and members of organizations of which we're a part.

The help they provide can come in many forms. Having a sympathetic ear to listen to us can be a great help in dealing with difficult situations. People that care about us often have valuable suggestions. The pressure we feel to fulfill our commitments to those we care about can be a valuable motivation. Those that care about us sometimes introduce us to other very helpful people, clients and employers.

It's important to be aware of the people that depend on us to do well and the various ways they can help us helps us be attuned to opportunities to move forward. If any of them ask what they can do to help, it's important to be able to tell them the specifics of what they can offer in an understandable manner.

Here are some examples of help I've received from invested parties.

My first job, other than working for my parents, was from someone who knew and liked me. She found me through my parents and offered me a job ahead of over 200 people who applied. Until the offer, I didn't even know the job existed.

Often, I get calls from prospective mortgage clients telling me they were referred to me by friends, relatives or co workers.

At one point I was struggling with how to re structure my business in response to a changing market. A good friend of mine gave me a suggestion that when I heard it, I knew it was the right path. I'd been working on the issue for a long time and was greatly relieved to see the path forward. I was confident it was the best choice.

Sadly, there are things I'll do for those I care about that I wouldn't do for myself even though they benefit us both.

It's important for us to make our self vulnerable, share what we need help with to those who care about us or have a vested interest in us doing well. I have a friend who is suffering greatly because he's too proud to share his difficulties with many who could and would help him. Don't be that person.

I once was in a very difficult spot and my efforts to return to a peaceful state were failing miserably. I called a friend and told him I really needed his help, would he meet with me, NOW. He dropped everything to meet and, with his help, I was able to return to a balanced clear state. I was once again confident in my abilities to make good decisions and move forward.

Let the people in our lives who are invested in us doing well, help us.

Chapter 9

Effectively Addressing Obstacles

"Being in a peaceful state allows us to see and implement solutions we otherwise couldn't"

Scott Friedman

Business could be viewed as problem solving. Everyone in business has encountered obstacles, sometimes a mountain of them in one day!!!

There are critical steps in effectively addressing obstacles. First and foremost, get clear on what the problem is. Too often I've felt the problem was infinite or too big to deal with. I've not wanted to deal with a great many problems. Many times I've told myself I don't know what to do about a problem . In every case, when I've gone to write the problem down in as honest terms as possible, the apparent magnitude of the problem was much smaller than I'd been telling myself. It turned out a big part of my problem is typically a fear my response to the problem won't effective. The more I articulate the problem, the clearer I get on what I can and cannot do to solve it.

If the definition of a problem is unresolved conflict, then resolving the conflict within myself solves my problem. Focusing on peace results in me being more effective in coming up with ideas about what I can do to create a successful outcome and do it. When I get to the point where I've done all I can, I accept that there's nothing more I can do. At that point a deal either works or it doesn't. Either way, if I've done everything in my power to have the deal work, I'm at peace and can move on.

Some obstacles I end up addressing from unanticipated perspectives. Marketing has long been a challenge/obstacle for me. Doing what others have done hasn't worked well for me. What does work for me is acting on ideas I strongly relate to working; ideas I believe in strongly enough. I believe that focusing on being in a peaceful state is the most effective thing I can do. I relate to harmonizing with peace creating beneficial opportunities in my life I couldn't create any other way. Recently, while engaged in focusing on peace, I was invited to give a graduation speech to a school I didn't even know existed. Again while focusing on peace, I got a call from a relative of a past client looking for a large loan.

It doesn't matter how we address obstacles, only that what we do works for us. It doesn't matter how conventional, unconventional or down right strange, as long as it works.

Chapter 10

When a Deal Doesn't Work

"I only have control over myself"

Scott Friedman

This is the real world, not everything works the way we wish it would.

When a deal doesn't work, we should always see what we can learn from this to be more effective next time. I find once I've extracted what I can learn from a situation, I can let it go and move on.

In many cases when I don't "get the deal" it's because I've held back being myself. Even after decades of experience proving it otherwise, part of me still believes if I share with people my spiritual and global perspectives and how they integrate with our deal, they'll run the other way. Sometimes that keeps me from making the depth of connection that would result in the client deciding to move forward with me.

I was meeting with a judge who was buying a new house following his divorce. We discussed his situation and I offered a few solutions to his circumstance of not having a 20% down payment readily available, how to handle not having the mortgage on the past residence count in his debt ratio and several other technical and procedural obstacles. What I didn't do was share with him the books I've written, the speeches I've made and my commitment and strategy to improving our society. In retrospect, I believe, as a judge, he would have appreciated that. I believe it would have impacted his decision to work with me. As it was he went with someone who offered a tiny bit lower price which maybe they could deliver and maybe they couldn't. With a deeper relationship I believe we would have found a way to work together. In the mortgage business it occurs far too often that people offer pricing they can't deliver on. The fact that "bait and switch" is illegal does little to deter some.

A friend of mine was buying a home and the optimal loan for him was a type I don't frequently do. Instead of doing what I did with another friend in the identical situation after that, I told him to go to someone with more experience with that type of loan. With my second friend I realized I can figure out any type of loan and the negotiating and advocacy skills I have are applicable with all loans. The difference was my acceptance of the fact that even if I don't have a lot of experience with a specific loan or deal, I have the skills to learn what I need to know to get the job done and done well.

It's ok not every deal works. As long as we can learn what to do differently to be more effective next time, it's not a total loss.

Chapter 11

Being Clear on What We Bring to the Table

"If we don't think well of our self, how can we expect others to?" – Scott Friedman

Being arrogant is believing we're better than other people Being confident is taking ownership of our skills and abilities. **In order to fully utilize and benefit from our talents, we have to take ownership of them.** If we don't think well of ourselves, how do we expect others to?

Believing in our self is probably the greatest of all skills and attributes. When we believe in our self it opens the door for others to believe in us too. The best method I've found to increase our belief in our self is to ask our self the question, "If I believed in myself one increment more than I now do, what would I do?" and then do it. Answering this question has resulted in me writing books, taking on consulting work and investing in myself.

It's not enough to accept the talent we have. We must also accept the value we have for others. **We're not better or worse than other people simply because we have a different skill set.**

There are two categories of needs people have; needs they're focused on and needs common to us all. To bring the maximum value possible to the table we must fulfill as many of the client's needs as possible.

The needs my clients are focused on are solving a problem before them. The problem could be obtaining a mortgage, solving a people problem at work, viewing their employment circumstances more accurately so they can make better career decisions or any of a wide array of problems. The deeper problems we all share are how to be more at peace, more accepting of our self, and what is true. As with all leadership, **the most effective form of leadership is example.**

Being at peace around other people is of tremendous value. I have a friend who gets brilliant inspiration after brilliant inspiration when we get together. Because I present a peaceful centered state the impediments to him receiving inner inspiration get relaxed. **People think more clearly, more effectively and more creatively when they're in a peaceful centered environment.**

Once I had a friend who asked for my help because she felt she was stuck in a terrible situation. I gifted her money to get out and instructed her to go stay with her family, people who love her. I told her to forget about whether they understood her or not. All that mattered was for her to be in the environment of people who love her. Then, in that environment, I explained, she would be able to think clearly and make a good decision for the next phase of her life. Next I heard, she was enrolled in graduate school in a different state and doing very well.

We are of value more for who we are and how we are than for what we do. Certainly what we do matters and is affected by who we are AND who we are has much greater value and impact than what we do. I select the people I associate with far more based on who they are than what they do.

The more I identify with being peace and light, the greater value I am to individuals and the world in total.

Chapter 12

The Importance of a Clear Conscience

"The truth comes out eventually" – Scott Friedman

It's been said, and I agree, the average person can detect insincerity from across a crowed room. Too often in business people are afraid to fully disclose all the facts because they fear it will kill the deal. Exactly the opposite is true; not disclosing everything is more likely to kill the deal than anything else.

Under disclosing, over promising and misrepresenting destroy peace of mind, trust. That trust is needed to have the working relationship needed to solve problems that arise.

There have been a great many deals that were in trouble that got saved because the truth was fully and accurately disclosed in the beginning.

An underwriter called to say he was not approving a loan because the income was too low in relation to the debt. I sent back my calculations based on the initial submission that had the ratio in the acceptable range. I asked him to reply in writing where his numbers varied from mine. He changed his numbers to match mine and approved the loan. This only works when we completely and accurately present the facts.

I explain to my mortgage clients the process, the criteria and how their criteria match up against the lenders'. Then I make clear this is the real world and anything can happen. They commit to address any unforeseen issues that may arise in a teamwork manner to get the best result. Usually there are no issues, and on occasion there are. Because I haven't over promised, I don't have to be embarrassed if a problem arises. I promise to give my full attention and maximum effort to getting the job done. This I have control over and can do.

My clients know this is the real world and appreciate being told the truth. It engenderers greater trust and confidence on their part. The clearer my conscience the more at peace I am and the more secure my clients are that their interests are being well represented.

Chapter 13

Fair Fees

"What is fair is best for everyone" – Scott Friedman

Win/win thinking embraces the fact that fair is best for everyone.

Charging too much leaves the seller feeling guilty and the buyer being taken unfair advantage of. Charging too little leaves the seller angry and disrespected while the buyer becomes nervous about the commitment of the seller to follow through.

What is fair is usually a subjective range. It's incumbent for people of good character to have a good faith discussion in determining what is fair. As always, **the degree of peace we feel is a reliable measure of how fair things are.**

My objective in every deal is to provide the maximum value I can. That frequently includes explaining the advantages and disadvantages of various options. In determining the optimal loan the relative importance of the needs of the client must be discerned. Some of the considerations are, interest paid, monthly payment, cash required, time to complete the deal, risk tolerance, time the loan is expected to remain in place and ability to budget. Most borrowers aren't aware they have the option to make a one time lump sum principal reduction and have the monthly payment lowered on a fixed rate loan. Many borrowers don't realize they can choose to have or not have an escrow account for taxes, or insurance or both on most loans. The value contributed impacts a fair price.

Unforeseen obstacles can occur in a deal. I've had to resolve the county having conflicting property addresses in their records; liens not belonging to my clients appearing on credit or title reports; IRS refusing to validate tax returns due to increased security after being previously hacked. After an earthquake, I had to get certification from a state licensed engineer that the house was safe to inhabit before the lenders would fund a loan. Once a borrower changed her mind and asked me to help stop a purchase after they'd signed all the documents and the loan had funded. The title company was about to record the transfer of title. I walked her through it. Many times I've procured loans for people turned down by others by structuring the loan differently and finding the right lender. In some cases I've funded the loan through the lender that previously turned the loan down. I've advised my clients on what to do to raise their credit score thereby qualifying for a better loan. There seems to be no end of obstacles that can arise. Solving the problems that would otherwise kill a deal has obvious value.

I monitor past client's loans and if the market presents the opportunity to lower their rate without any points or fees to the borrower, I make that available. My fee and all the other costs are paid by a credit from the lender. For example, in one case the rate on a 15 year loan with the client paying all the costs was 2.5% when rates were near their lowest. At 2.875% interest rate there was a credit from the lender that paid all the costs. This was still a lower interest rate than was currently being paid. The client lowered their rate, paid no points or fees, and because of that had no costs to recoup before beginning to enjoy the savings of the lower rate. Additionally, if the rate dropped further in the future they could repeat the process.

One client intends to hold the property for the rest of his life. Because the longer a loan is in place, the more important the interest rate is and the less important are the fees. He chose to pay many thousands of dollars in additional fees to "buy" a lower rate. He wanted the security of a low fixed rate. That was more important to him than the fees or how many years it would take for the fees to be compensated for by the lower rate.

Once I misquoted a client. I told him about my mistake and gave him the option of going forward with the quoted rate or paying an additional $17/mo for what the rate should have been. I made it clear I would do whatever he decided and would never bring it up again. He wanted the original quote. That's what he got. In this case what was fair was to keep my word at the cost of my fee. That was years ago and I haven't made that mistake since!! After that loan, he referred me several other borrowers.

What's fair is impacted by the value received, the market and the particular parameters of the situation. We know we're being fair when everyone feels good about the deal. **If people choose to work together again, that's a clear sign the previous deal was fair.**

Chapter 14

Be Proud of the Effort

"I'm at peace when I know I've done my best"
Scott Friedman

There is only a moment when the deal is done. The bulk of our time and effort is spent in the process of the deal. For too many of us too much of our attention is focused on the outcome and not enough on the current moment.

Once again, "Peace" is a wonderfully effective guide and measure. Only when I've done all that is appropriate in moving a deal forward, am I at peace. If it's the weekend and the people I need to talk to in order to move things forward are unavailable until Monday, I can write the activity on my Monday list and be at peace over the weekend.

When I've done all I can for now, I'm at peace. Part of being at peace is being proud of my effort and behavior. I've done my best to structure the deal so it works for everyone. I've given thought to what problems could arise and done what I can to minimize or eliminate those problems in advance. I've honestly, fairly and creatively addressed the situations as they arise. All that and more I can rest assured have taken place if I'm at peace. If I'm not at peace, it's usually a sign there is constructive action appropriate for me to take now. The questions I ask myself often is, "Have I done all I can do at this time?"

Being proud of my efforts is an important part of being at peace. Sometimes it's amazing how productive being at peace is…

I was working on a loan that an underwriter declined, approved and then declined. I had to keep calming my anger so I could think of the next thing to try to get the loan approved. Effort after effort failed. Eventually I ran out of ideas and no one else had any either. I accepted I'd done all I could to get the loan done and it just wasn't going to happen. The lender makes a big deal of wanting to learn from its mistakes and make them right. I found out the e mail address to share all that I thought was wrong with how the loan was handled. When they called me to hear what I had to say, I was calm and emphasized I was only doing this because I took them at their word that they were always looking to improve. Much to my surprise, the man took it upon himself to investigate the loan. Three hours later he called me with loan approval without me ever having asked for his help. I'd accepted it wasn't going to work before I spoke to him. My efforts to stay calm were effective in getting a deal done where all the overt, trying this, trying that, had failed. I was both proud of my effort to stay at peace (not always successfully…) and excited that had beneficial practical deal making effects.

When the mortgage industry was making loans to people who couldn't pay them back, I refused to do that. It cost me a lot of money in lost fees. I just couldn't in good conscience put someone into a loan they couldn't pay. When loans began defaulting in record numbers, loans I made didn't have problems. When others fled or were run out of the mortgage industry, I'm still here. When others hid from borrowers they put into problematic loans, I got repeat business and referrals from past clients. When others were contacted with demands to repurchase fraudulent loans, I've never had that happen. I am proud of my efforts to prosper by doing the right thing.

Once I was working on a reverse mortgage. Obstacle after obstacle kept coming up and the client asked me if I thought the loan would get made. I assured him we'd solved all the prior obstacles and I'd put however much energy it took to resolve the current and any other hurdles. I was confident I had the strength to get the loan done. I did. I was proud of the energy, commitment and expertise I employed to make the deal work. I only take on loans I believe in and I put everything I have into getting them done. I am proud of the level of effort I make on behalf of my clients.

On one loan the appraisal came in below the purchase price and I felt it shouldn't have. I got more accurate comparable sales from an appraiser I'd worked with in the past. I presented these comparable sales with an explanation of why they were more representative of the value of the house being purchased. Often people don't like to admit having made a mistake. Appraisers tend to be very much that way. I pushed and pushed and eventually got the appraisal changed and the loan closed. Again, I was proud of my effort.

In doing a deal often times it's necessary to point out with ever greater clarity what is true. For that to be effective, the deal has to be good for everyone. If everyone is better off doing the deal, that needs to be made clear. As obvious as it sounds, there are times when it takes a Herculean effort. Although, the more I can stay calm in the process, the smoother and faster problems get resolved and deals made. Choosing to remain calm over getting angry when people are close minded, wrong and committed to their mistakes can be a real challenge. I am proud of my increasing ability to choose staying calm and at peace.

Being proud of the efforts we make, how we conduct ourselves, is an important part in making deals work for everyone.

Chapter 15

Drawing Strength

"Aligning with the truth is an unlimited source of strength"
Scott Friedman

All strength is ultimately moral strength.

The truth is an inexhaustible source of power. The calmer we are, the more evident the truth becomes. Everyone is better off knowing and accepting the truth even though at the time we may not like it.

When I'm working with a client I ask them to tell me everything they think could be pertinent because I need a full deck if I'm going to be the best possible advocate for them. I'm fond of telling clients, "I'm much better at solving problems I know about than problems I don't know about".

Too often people try to hide the truth because they believe it will be detrimental to them if others know the truth. That is a recipe for disaster. **Truth has a way of making itself known**.

In conversations sometimes I'll start with a general statement of truth to frame the perspective and lend support to an enhanced acceptance of the details of truth in the specific situation. Sometimes I'll say, "We all want things to go well. If you have a good experience, I will too." Then, often times, I get into how important it is for clients to ask questions and voice concerns. Another way I use a statement of truth to gain strength is to say, "I have bad news to convey which I wish I didn't. AND, I feel I have an obligation to tell you the truth". Then I give the bad news and a suggestion for how to best respond to it.

A client of mine was getting divorced and part of the agreement was she refinance her house so both title and the loan were in her name only. She had a deadline to accomplish this, or the house would have to be sold. To qualify she needed to count her alimony as income. I found a lender who would credit the alimony income after 3 months of receiving it as compared to all the other lenders requirement of 6 months. She didn't have 6 months. People were quoting ridiculously low rates. I made sure she asked them how many months she had to have received alimony for it to count. In every case it was 6 months, too long for her situation. Had that truth not been highlighted she might have wasted valuable time applying unsuccessfully to banks who wouldn't close her loan in time. Keeping people focused on the truth is often instrumental in getting deals done.

There is tremendous strength in highlighting and focusing on the truth. Sadly, as obvious as this is, it's too frequently not practiced.

Conclusion

We all have unique abilities and knowledge. The ethical deal is valuing what we and others have to contribute for our mutual benefit, and making it happen.

Afterword

Scott Friedman has been a mortgage broker for over 30 years. In that time he's had ample opportunity to test out the efficacy of his principles in real life business situations.

In addition to continuing as a mortgage broker, he his now offering the benefit of his experience as a consultant to business and government, a public speaker and author.

For more information or to contact Scott go to Visirity.com or e mail to scott@visirity.com .